Movies Are Us

G. Beverly Wells, Ph.D.

Also by G. Beverly Wells

Books
Pieces of Three
Falling Leaves
Stuttering Treatment: A Comprehensive Clinical Guide
Effect of Certain Aspects of Syntax on Stuttering
Effects of Adult Attachment Style and Lesbian Identity
Integration on Internalized Shame

Contributions to Books
New Voices in American Poetry
73 Poets Anthology
Lesbian and Bisexual Women's Mental Health
Reader's Guide to Lesbian and Gay Studies
Test Critiques
Colloquium of Communication Disorders
Linguistics in Oklahoma

Articles in Professional Journals
Journal of Psychology and Human Sexuality
Journal of Homosexuality
The California Psychologist
Journal of Fluency Disorders
Linguistics Proceedings
Communicative Disorders
Journal of the Iowa Speech and Hearing Association
Proceedings of the Mid-America Linguistics Conference
Journal of the Acoustical Society of America
Journal of the Missouri Speech and Hearing Association

Acknowledgments

I want to thank Jackie Zilbach, Genevieve Howe, and John Gladfelter for inspiring the research that eventually led to this book

Movies Are Us
Three Classic Films

Author Photo by Bonnie M. Burroughs

Second Edition 2016
ISBN:9781533018380

Printed in the United States of America

For

Genevieve

Contents

Introduction

Movies not only entertain us, but they also have the ability to reflect human behavior and the power to impact how we behave. They can reflect how we see ourselves and others, as well as how we view the world in general. Films provide us with fantasies that both reflect and embellish our visions of the world.

At their best, movies that become classic films achieve universality and a pure state of art that deeply affects the audience. Classic films, such as the ones discussed in this book are complicated works of art often involving a number of varied and interlocking pieces within the overall theme. From these three classic films, I have selected particular pieces which lend themselves to psychological study.

In David Mamet's *House of Games,* I have chosen to focus on the character of Dr. Ford, a psychiatrist. In Part I, I first examine her manifestations of burnout impairment while finally focusing on the development of Dr. Ford as a criminal personality.

In Part II, I conduct a Jungian analysis of the individuation of David Burton, the main character in Peter Weir's, *The Last Wave.* To better understand this complex film and David Burton's individuation process, attention is given to both Jungian principles and the spiritual mysteries of the Australian Aborigines.

Finally, Part III studies the social psychological issues of stereotypes and group development in John Hughes, *The Breakfast Club*. In this film, each character represents a different stereotype. Despite this, they manage to form group cohesion without benefit of a group leader.

Part I: *House of Games*
Director: David Mamet

Plot and Major Characteristics

Margaret Ford, M.D., is a successful psychiatrist and best-selling author of a book entitled, *Driven*, a study of compulsive and addictive behaviors. Although seemingly devoted to her patients, she pursues her work in a mechanical, intellectualized manner. Her appearance is androgynous with short, severely cut hair and figure-hiding business suits.

She chain smokes unfiltered Camels throughout the film and is presented as a driven individual, addicted to work and tobacco. Two of her patients are troubling her. One is a young woman who is incarcerated in the prison wing of the hospital for murder. The other is Billy, a young man who compulsively gambles. As the plot unfolds, we learn that both patients pose a challenge to her sense of professional competence.

Dr. Ford turns to her elderly mentor, Dr. Maria Littauer, to share her concerns about her work. Dr. Littauer is sympathetic and counsels her to work less and find time to relax. In a therapy session, Billy reveals that he owes a professional gambler $25,000, and if it is not paid soon, he will be killed. Further, he taunts her by saying that the therapy is "just talk, just talk. The whole thing is a con game, you do nothing." In response, Dr. Ford promises to do whatever is necessary to help.

Later that evening she makes the decision to directly intervene. She resolves to go to the "House of Games" to meet the professional gambler, Mike, to whom Billy owes the money. She believes she can convince Mike to erase Billy's debt.

At the "House of Games" she finds Mike, the confidence man into whose clutches she will fall. He assures her that he will forgive Billy's debt if she will assist him by watching for a "tell," an unconscious mannerism that will indicate that his poker game opponent is bluffing. She appears to become intellectually and sexually excited by Mike.

Dr. Ford returns to the "House of Games" again. She proposes to Mike that he allow her to make a study of confidence men by observing him and his colleagues. He consents to her offer. As the film unfolds, she is irresistibly drawn to Mike and ends up in bed with him. In response to her question, "What do you think I want?" Mike responds, I'll tell you. Somebody to come along, somebody to possess you, to take you into a new thing."

Following that, Dr. Ford accompanies Mike as an elaborate "long con" game unfolds. The following day she realizes that she, not the "target," has been the intended victim of a brilliantly conceived and executed confidence game. Not only was the "target" an accomplice, but so was Billy, the young patient that she had gone to such extraordinary lengths to "rescue" from his gambling addiction.

Later, Dr. Ford tracks Mike down and confronts him. There is an acrimonious interchange, and she eventually shoots and kills him. In the final scene of the film, she is wearing sunglasses, hoop earrings, and a floral print dress while having lunch with Dr. Littauer, after returning from what she has described as a relaxing long vacation.

While Dr. Littauer is briefly absent from the table, Margaret Ford takes the opportunity to steal a lighter from the woman at the next table. As she lights her cigarette, a look of great satisfaction crosses her face, apparently from this small feat of criminal behavior.

Dr. Ford as Impaired Psychiatrist

In the early scenes of the film, "House of Games," we observe signs of impairment from burnout on the part of the main character, Margaret Ford, M.D. Dr. Ford presents with many of the most common psychological and behavioral signals to the presence of burnout, as described by Freudenberger (1975). One of the primary signs we see is the tendency to over-identify with her patients.

Another sign is over commitment and enmeshment in work to the point of losing herself. We observe that Dr. Ford appears to have no other life or friendships, apart from her mentor, with the entire focus of her life on her work with patients.

As the plot unfolds we see Dr. Ford taking on feelings of omnipotence that lead her to dangerous risk taking behavior, i.e., placing herself in the "House of Games," a situation too dangerous for her to handle. Individuals experiencing burnout are also likely to engage in addictive drugs and/or behaviors. Dr. Ford smokes and works excessively, at what one might term, an addictive level.

An individual like Dr. Ford, who engages in addictive behaviors, increases the likelihood of another burnout symptom, that of increased rigidity and defensiveness. Rigidity and defensiveness decrease even more the probability of a favorable response to the informal peer suggestion of Dr. Littauer to relax and take needed time away from work. Another related sign of burnout identified by Freudenberger (1975) is the development of a cynical attitude toward being able to help her patients while spending more hours at work with less productivity.

Dr. Ford, in addition to her private practice, works in an institution (hospital locked ward), which has been found to promote higher levels of the kinds of stressors that lead to burnout. Therapeutic work, itself, has been found to expose the therapist to high levels of both depersonalization and emotional exhaustion (Ackerley, et al. 1988; Masloch Burnout Inventory (MBI) 1986). Hellman, et al. (1986) also found that therapeutic work exposes therapists to five distinct stressors, including maintenance of the therapeutic relationship, scheduling difficulties, professional doubt, work over-involvement, and personal depletion.

The film introduces us to the burnout profile of Dr. Margaret Ford as she autographs her best-selling book, *Driven*, for an admirer. The only friend we are introduced to is one professional colleague, a mentor of Dr. Ford's. We see nothing of any other friends or family members. The film presents Dr. Ford's life as consisting solely of her work, providing direct therapy services to patients in a locked ward and in a private practice setting.

Like her book title, we quickly see evidence that Dr. Ford is "driven." She leaves the female murderer in the locked ward and joins her colleague in a restaurant for lunch, saying "I'm sorry I'm late," and proceeds to discuss with pride, the uncovering work she has just done with her patient. She then tells her colleague, "I don't have time" (for lunch). As Dr. Ford continues to speak, she says, "Sometimes I think the way pressures in my life are…," while her colleague, Dr. Littauer, directs Dr. Ford's attention to her substitution of "pressures" for "pleasures".

"Many things that should be pleasures are pressures, says Dr. Littauer. "Listen to me. Slow down. Try to enjoy yourself…" Dr. Ford responds initially with a look of confusion, perhaps reflecting her own apparent confusion in her life between "pressures" and "pleasures". Her colleague admonishes her with, "Your friend asks you to lunch; eat lunch with her." To which Dr. Ford replies, "Do you forgive me?" "Goodbye. Go work," responds Dr. Littauer, and Dr. Ford leaves without lunch.

As the film unfolds, we see Dr. Ford in her office with Billy, a compulsive gambler. He challenges her by saying, "What the hell do you know, man? You're rich. You're comfortable. You've got your Goddam book you wrote. All the time you want to help me, you don't do dick, man." "You want to help me? Help me with this (pulling out a gun). Because if not, I've got to use it to kill myself." Dr. Ford becomes actively engaged with the challenge, saying, "Billy, Billy, I swear to you. You give me the gun, and I will help you."

Summary

The film, *House of Games*, reveals the profile of Dr. Margaret Ford as a professional who is overinvolved with her work to the detriment of a personal or social life. We see instances in which she over-identifies with her patients and is too busy to participate in a luncheon engagement with her friend and mentor. She also fails to respond to her colleague's concern about her overwork and lack of balance in her life.

Dr. Ford demonstrates seven of the common signs of burnout identified by Freudenberger (1975). They include (1) over-commitment to work, with a belief in self-success tied to dedication and successful work involvement; (2) enmeshment in work to the point of losing herself; (3) not taking space/time for herself socially; (4) a tendency to over-identify with patients, a reflection of loss of self; (5) rigidity as exemplified in her being closed to input from her mentor regarding overwork, and her resistance to change; (6) nicotine as an addictive substance, e.g., chain smoking, and work as an addictive all-consuming behavior; and (7) feelings of omnipotence, leading to risk taking behavior, placing herself and her patients in potential danger. Finally, the film reveals that Dr. Ford is not following the recommendations of Keith-Spiegel and Koocher (1985) for preventative actions in crisis situations.

Development of Dr. Ford's Criminal Personality

In the earlier section the focus of the discussion was on the issues and signs of burnout exhibited by Dr. Margaret Ford, the main character in Mamet's *House of Games*, thus leading to her impairment as a psychiatrist. This section assesses her behavior through the application of the seminal volumes of research findings of Yochelson and Samenow (1993) on the characteristics and development of the criminal personality.

This discussion will focus on criminal thinking patterns and automatic errors of thinking, including those related to the crime, criminal tactics, and criminal use of common terms and the phases of development of criminal behavior as applied to Dr. Ford in the film. Yochelson and Samenow (1993) use the term, "criminal" to describe a person who has "*thinking processes* that an irresponsible but non-arrestable person, the petty thief, and the 'professional' criminal all manifest, but to different degrees and with different consequences" (p. 253). Early in the film we see Dr. Ford with a female patient, followed by a brief meeting with a colleague. In these scenes we observe what seems to be "responsible" behavior.

Dr. Ford appears next with Billy, a patient who is a compulsive gambler. He pulls out a gun and threatens suicide due to fears about the debt he owes

Mike at the "House of Games." She says to him, "Give me the gun, and I will help you."

She later goes to the "House of Games" and tells Mike, "You threatened a friend of mine. That behavior doesn't go." She agrees to participate in a *con,* conscious deception in a card game, in return for cancellation of Billy's gambling debt. Her behavior has now moved into the category of "irresponsible" but "non-arrestable" behavior.

Later in the film Dr. Ford willingly participates in more *cons,* one involving having sex with Mike in what she believes to be someone else's hotel room and taking a jackknife as a souvenir; and a later situation in which she believes that, with Mike and his buddy, Joey, she is involved in another criminal operation. At these points she has moved along the continuum to the level of "arrestable criminal behavior."

Near the end of the film when she plans the *con* and murder of Mike, she has moved into the realm of "extreme criminal" behavior. Although Mamet does not provide us with direct information on Dr. Ford's way of life from childhood, he does take the viewer through her progress as a "criminal" with a variety of behaviors along the continuum from "responsible" to "irresponsible non-arrestable" to "arrestable criminal," and finally to "extreme criminal" behavior.

Although we have no direct knowledge of her past, a recurring theme, literal and/or symbolic, appears in the film around the effect of the term, "whore" on Dr. Ford. We first see this when she is counseling the murderess who uses the term, with the implication being that the person she murdered may have been her father, who called her a "whore." During this scene, Dr. Ford seems to resonate with her distress and even comforts her.

Following this session, she meets with her mentor, Dr. Littauer. Distressed, Dr. Ford says, cynically, that therapy is like a con game, that she really can't do anything to help the murderess. Dr. Ford then says, "My father called me a whore." "*Your* father called you a whore?" responds Dr. Littauer. Dr. Ford does not respond to this query. Later in the film, just before she fires the fatal bullets into Mike, the theme comes full circle when Mike says, "You're a whore, you son of a bitch."

According to Yochelson and Samenow (1993), the criminal is tremendously energetic. Likewise, Dr. Ford does appear to have boundless energy. She has written and published a highly successful book; she has a private practice and sees patients in a locked facility while she also finds time to learn the "con game" from Mike. Yochelson and Samenow (1993, p. 258) also state that "if the criminal were free to do as he wanted, his energy would suddenly be present and observable even after exhausting work." Dr. Ford appears to have almost limitless reserves of energy; after a day of professional activity, she seems energized by an evening of criminal activity.

"Fears in the criminal are widespread, persistent, and intense" (Yochelson and Samenow, 1993, p. 258); however, the criminal can eliminate fear long enough to do what s/he wants, i.e. to commit a crime. Dr. Ford does seem fearless as she engages in criminal activity. When she believes she is responsible for the murder of a policeman, her fear of being apprehended soars to a conscious level, and she says, "I can't be here." Her fear in this instance is in sharp contrast to the fearlessness she has conveyed in other dangerous situations.

Another characteristic of the criminal personality identified by Yochelson and Samenow (1993) is the all-encompassing fear of being a "zero" or being in the "zero state." The criminal fears being reduced to a "nothing." The "zero state" has three components: (1) the overall image of being a nothing; (2) "transparency," in which the criminal believes that everyone sees him this way; and (3) "permanence," in which the criminal believes that this zero state will never change (p. 266).

Evidence for this "all or none" kind of thinking, being either grandiose or a zero is evident in the film sequence when Dr. Ford says to Billy, "Give me the gun and I will help you." After telling her the danger he's in, Billy retorts, "What kind of help is your damn promise now?" This puts her in danger of the feared zero state. That evening she goes to the

"House of Games" and tells Mike, "You threatened my friend. That behavior doesn't go. Talk turkey, pal."

Later in the film she discovers she has been conned when she overhears Mike and his cohorts saying, "Took her money and screwed her too" as they split up the money. In danger of being a zero, she makes plans to get back at Mike and cons him. During their last interchange while holding a gun on him, she says to Mike, "Beg for your life or I'm going to kill you." Outwitting him and reducing him to a zero in the end allows her to move out of the dangerous zero state.

Anger and pride in the criminal personality is also evident in the scenes just cited. The criminal is chronically angry. When Dr. Ford, like other criminals, doesn't get her way as when Mike and his cronies con her the last time, she becomes vulnerable to being in the zero state and seeks angry retribution. Criminal pride is in the inflexibly high self-evaluation, the grandiose state that Dr. Ford manifests as she threatens Mike initially at the "House of Games" and when she tells him to beg for his life later in the film.

The "power thrust" characteristic of the criminal personality is manifested throughout the film with Dr. Ford always seeking to be number one. The power thrust is observable even in her nonverbal behavior while signing her book in the opening of the film and her report to her mentor of how she deciphered what the murderess really meant. In these instances the message being conveyed is "all sorts of people tell me 'You're smart.'" (Yochelson and Samenow, 1993, p. 278.

Dr. Ford's greatest excitement, like other criminals, is doing the forbidden and getting away with it. The excitement shows clearly in her change of expression to bright eyes and smiles as she successfully executes a forbidden act, whether it's stealing the jackknife in the hotel room tryst or successfully getting away with Mike's murder or stealing the cigarette lighter from a woman in the restaurant.

Genuine religious sentimentality and self-seeking use of religion have been identified as part of the criminal personality. However, the film does not provide evidence of sentimentality on the part of Dr. Ford.

Concrete thinking patterns also have been found to be characteristic of the criminal personality. Dr. Ford evidences some of this when she fully believes, because she saw the "tell" Mike asked her to watch for in the card game, that it definitely meant the other man was bluffing. She says, "He played with his ring. Call the bet; I'll back it up. If he loses, I'll write you a check."

Like other criminals, Dr. Ford appears to see her crimes as a series of actions that are unrelated. To her they are triumphs, proof that she is number one.

She, like other criminals, does not conceptualize herself as a criminal. Life is a series of conquests, rather than degrees of criminal behavior (Yochelson and Samenow, 1993).

Fragmentation is another characteristic of the criminal personality that has been described by the researchers in which inconsistencies in behavior are obvious. We see such inconsistencies with Dr. Ford. On the one hand, she can comfort and provide therapy services, ostensibly to help people, and in the next moment, she can do things like steal, con, or even kill another human being.

Uniqueness is another characteristic of the criminal personality, but not in the usual sense of the word. It is the belief that she is superior to others. This belief leads the criminal to refuse to submit to anyone. "To do so is to lose his identity." (Yochelson, and Samenow, 1993, p.317). Dr. Ford demonstrates this when she is determined not to submit to Mike in their initial encounter, and of course, in the end in dramatic fashion, when she exacts fatal retribution from Mike, rather than to submit to his "use" of her.

A professional criminal is perfectionistic in the things he values and chooses, and particularly so when it comes to planning and executing the perfect crime. He is also perfectionistic, according to the researchers, in his readiness to accuse others of immoral behavior. Dr. Ford is perfectionistic in her planning and execution of the conning and killing of

Mike, down to the last detail. She also accuses him of immoral behavior. As she points the gun at him, she says, "You used me."

The criminal is "impervious to suggestions" when others want him to change but highly suggestible when he is looking for action (Yochelson and Samenow, 1993). She responds rigidly to her mentor's suggestions to socialize with her and find enjoyable things to do, yet she is highly suggestible when she has the opportunity to get involved with Mike's action. Also, when her mentor suggests that she do something that gives her pleasure, she interprets it as a criminal would, and thinks of the excitement of doing something forbidden.

A criminal is a loner in that he lacks affectionate relationships but will be gregarious with other criminals. A "friend" is someone who will "do what the criminal wants" or "someone who will not jeopardize him" or an "acquaintance." (Yochelson and Samenow, 1993, p. 525). Dr. Ford, seeking excitement, power, and perfectionism, goes to the "House of Games" and referring to Billy, says to Mike, "You threatened my friend."

Throughout the film, Dr. Ford is not engaged in any warm, affectionate relationships. Even with her colleague, she appears distant and disconnected. However, after almost getting conned in the card game by Mike and his cronies, she visits with them outside on the street, smiling and engaged.

The criminal is active sexually, but the focus is less on sensuality than it is on the "power, the conquest, the buildup, and the triumph" of being irresistible. Indirect reference to being called a whore by her father suggests the possibility that Dr. Ford, like other criminals, may have acted out sexually at an early age. However, that is speculative. In the film, she becomes sexually involved with Mike as a part of the excitement and sense of power and conquest involved in executing a crime together.

Another characteristic of the criminal personality is lying. For the criminal, lying is habitual and may be used as a way of building up his sense of self or to achieve an objective. A common and effective criminal technique is to tell part of the truth.

After she has murdered Mike and has returned from a time away after the murder, Dr. Ford alludes to her mentor's statement earlier in the film, "When you do something unforgivable, forgive yourself. You didn't kill anybody." Lying by omission, Dr. Ford says, both to herself and to her mentor, "You said I should forgive myself."

Here she lies (omitting the fact that she did kill someone) to achieve the goal of maintaining her image as a good person who is forgiven for a misstep. When she autographs a copy of her book near the end of the film, she writes in it, "Forgive yourself." As well as lying to achieve an objective, this could be looked at as another example of concrete thinking.

Yochelson and Samenow (1993), in their discussion of the criminal's automatic errors of thinking, mention that the criminal operates on the basis of a "closed channel." Dr. Ford seems to operate on such a basis, that is, she is secretive, has a closed mind except to criminal excitement, and is self-righteous. Although she and Mike are clearly both criminals using people with no concern for them as human beings, she says, accusingly, "You used me."

Some other automatic errors of thinking evident in Dr. Ford's behavior include: failure to put herself in another person's position in all of the non-arrestable and arrestable crimes, failure to be concerned about injuring others, and failure to assume obligations and responsible acts. When she expresses distress, it is only of being apprehended and not about concern for other people.

She also demonstrates what Yochelson and Samenow (1993) refer to as "ownership." In other words, if she wants something, like the cigarette lighter, she seems to believe that she is justified in stealing it. She glowed with triumph after the theft of the lighter.

Some of the characteristics of the criminal personality have to do with the execution of the crime, itself. Like other criminals, Dr. Ford responds to external (fear of getting caught) and internal (conscience) deterrents through "corrosion" and "cutoff." Corrosion refers to the mental process that allows her to slowly eliminate the deterrents from her mind until the desire to commit the crime outweighs the fears, and she can cut off the deterrents mentally, freeing herself to commit the crime.

As the corrosion process occurs, super optimism develops. In the case of the con and murder of Mike, she seems to have arrived at a place of certainty that things would go as planned. No re-emergence of the fear of getting caught appears as it did earlier when she thought she had killed the man in the hotel room. Fear seemed to be completely eradicated during Mike's execution. Like other professional criminals, Dr. Ford did not con or kill Mike on impulse. She carefully planned it and was in control of the event.

In short, Dr. Ford seems to view herself as a good and powerful person who does not need to follow any moral imperatives like others do, and who deserves to forgive herself and not be punished for any of her actions. As with other criminals, she minimizes and denies what she does not want to see. In a conversation with Mike after having sex in the hotel room, her denial is apparent. She says, "Some people would say that you're an interesting person."

"I'm a con man, that's what I am; I'm a criminal. "You don't have to delude yourself. You can call yourself what you are," says Mike. Later, when Mike and his buddies are dividing up Dr. Ford's money, referring to her one says, "The bitch is a born thief, man."

While studying Dr. Ford's behavior by applying psychological research findings on the criminal personality, it has become clear that she displays the vast majority of the characteristics of the criminal. During both arrestable and non-arrestable behavior, Dr. Ford reveals a developing and finally, a fully developed criminal personality.

References

Ackerley, Gary, Burnell, J., Holder, D., & Kurdek, L.(1988). Burnout among licensed psychologists. Professional Psychology: Research and Practice, 19 (6), 624-631.

Freudenberger, Herbert J. (1975). The staff burnout syndrome in alternative institutions. Psychotherapy Theory, Research, and Practice, 12 (1), 73-82.

Hellman, I., Morrison, T., & Abramowitz, S. (1986). The stresses of psychotherapeutic work: a replication and extension. Journal of Clinical Psychology, 42 (1), 197-205.

Keith-Spiegel, Patricia, & Koocher, Gerald. (1985). Ethics in psychology. San Francisco: McGraw-Hill.

Maslach, Christina, & Jackson, Susan. (1986). Maslach burnout inventory, second edition. Palo Alto: Consulting Psychologists Press.

Raquepaw, Jayne, & Miller, Rowland. (1989). Psychotherapist burnout: A componential analysis. Professional Psychology: Research and Practice, 20 (1), 32-36.

Yochelson, Samuel, & Samenow, Stanton. (1993/1976). The criminal personality Volume I: A profile for change. Northvale, N.J.: Jason Aronson.

Yochelson, Samuel, & Samenow, Stanton. (1994/1985). <u>The criminal personality Volume II: The change process.</u> Northvale, N.J.: Jason Aronson.

Yochelson, Samuel, & Samenow, Stanton. (1994/1986). <u>The criminal personality Volume III: The drug user.</u> Northvale, N.J.: Jason Aronson.

Part II: *The Last Wave*
Director: Peter Weir

Concept of Individuation

We travel with David Burton, the hero and main character in *The Last Wave*, on his individuating journey. *Individuation* is described by Jung as the full development of the individual's personality, which begins in mid-life. In mid-life, David Burton becomes aware of symbols that rise up out of his unconscious in dreams and reveal hidden psychological conflicts (Jung, 1973).

Jung (1959) differentiates the development of the individual personality from the *collective*, psychological contents that are not peculiar to a specific individual but to a society or mankind in general, i.e., "the mystical collective ideas" of the primitive (p.244). The collective character also includes whole functions, as thinking, feeling, sensation, and intuition.

David Burton begins his individuating journey with the conscious emergence of disturbing dreams and mysterious symbols and occurrences. We observe, throughout the film, the role of his unconscious leading to his self-realization. To come to full individuality we follow him through his process of reconciling opposite and contradictory aspects of his psyche. This process leads ultimately to his individuation.

Plot and Profile of David Burton

David Burton is a successful corporate taxation lawyer for a company in Sidney, Australia. He is white, in mid-life, financially successful with an established career, and apparently well-liked by friends and acquaintances. He has a seemingly calm, happy family life with his wife, Annie, and their two daughters. They live in a suburban home convenient to Sidney, where he works.

As his occupation suggests, his superior function seems to be his thinking. He appears calm, cerebral, and unemotional as he is introduced to us in the film. However, early on we discover that he is experiencing disturbing dreams. We also learn through a conversation with his stepfather that David had disturbing dreams as a child, including as is later revealed, a dream premonition of his mother's death.

David is asked to take on a legal case, a criminal case in which he is to defend five aborigines who are accused of killing a sixth aborigine in Sidney. Mystifying events occur, including a dream in which he sees an aborigine holding a sacred stone. He later meets Chris, the man in the dream, who turns out to be one of the aboriginal defendants.

Other bizarre events occur, such as black rain, huge hailstones, and water running out of the car radio. David's dilemma is that he is increasingly unable to find rational answers to the bizarre and mystical happenings. David learns from an anthropologist that there is a connection between the sacred stone and the aboriginal "dreamtime." As the film unfolds, he begins, more and more, to develop an affinity with the aborigines.

All this time David is developing a consciousness or awareness that draws upon other aspects of his psyche, including his feelings and intuition, which have been less accessible to him. Finally, Chris leads David through the sewers to underground caves containing aboriginal sacred objects. Here David seeks to obtain the wisdom of who he really is. The film ends, enigmatically with David on a beach, after he has fought his way back from the dark, subterranean regions to the redemptive light of the beach and the sight of a huge approaching wave.

Historical Background of the Screenplay

Peter Weir, in an interview with Judith Kass on January 8, 1979, offered some reflections of what was in his mind when he collaborated on the creation of the screenplay. Weir stated that the subject matter for the screenplay "just arose." He explained that he'd had a premonition when he was in Tunisia on a holiday, driving by Duga, an inland city that reminded him of Pompeii.

They stopped the car to exercise and as he returned, he had a feeling that he was going to find something. He was picking up stones and found one with parallel lines on it. When he pried it out of the earth, he found a skeleton of the head of a child.

He told Kass that it started him wondering about someone who thought precisely, like a lawyer, who dreamed about evidence and then found it through a premonition. Weir developed an outline of the screenplay, filling in much detail through the input of David Gulpilil, an aboriginal tribal man and film actor, a man with "a foot in both worlds," who played Chris in the film and Njiwarra Amagula, a tribal elder and clan leader, who played Charlie in the film.

Weir said that he had read the Old Testament, Velikovsky, the theories of Hyerdahl, and Castgeneda to find a new way to look at tribal people. He did not mention reading Jung as part of his research. During the interview Weir did, however, speak of the two primary male characters as opposites, "one white, one black; one tribal aborigine, one sophisticated western civilized man."

Weir elaborated. "One of them has material wealth; one has spiritual wealth. I wanted my lawyer… to, firstly, glimpse with his mind that there was another lost dream, or spiritual life, and then to touch it. In a sense, he's given a gift by the aborigines" (Kass, 1979, p.7).

Spiritual Mysteries of the Australian Aborigines

Spiritual activity is rarely detached from tribal ritual among the aborigines. The aborigine is brother to his kind, and his spiritual life is intimately connected with the collective spiritual life of his community. The inward *Dream Journey* is principally the exclusive preserve of men within the tribal community (Cowan, 1992).

The Dream Journey is a ritual act associated with making contact with a man's *Dreaming*, with his primordial ancestors, and with his *totem* or spiritual alter ego. It is only when a man makes this journey, either alone or with fellow initiates, that he begins to perceive his relationship with the spiritual powers embodied in his mythological heroes. Dreaming is a timeless reality that can be entered on earth. Myth and ritual are adjunct to this process. The real entry point is through transformation of the individual.

Cowan (1992) further explains that the aborigines, a nomadic people, project most of their inner beliefs onto their tribal landscape. The earth becomes a manifestation of a visionary geography, in which the soul can meet and converse with its higher power by way of symbolic expression. This means that the aboriginal initiate must mentally reconstitute the Dreaming here on earth if he wishes to attain a level of consciousness that allows him access to the Dreaming condition.

This is the reason why aboriginal earth or rock painting bears little similarity to the actual landscape of the tribal land. When the aborigine is painting his country or his Dreaming, he is not painting an actual physical landscape. He is painting a visionary landscape that conforms to the perception that has been handed down to him by his ancestors and satisfies his yearning for identification with his mythological heroes and his Dreaming ancestors.

The relationship between a man and his totem or a man to his Dreaming ancestor is not strictly a spiritual concept. It has a physical counterpart which embodies the spiritual mysteries. According to myth, at the time of creation of the world, the *Sky Heroes* wandered together across Australia, giving form to the land as they went (Cowan, 1992).

These Sky Heroes (spirit beings) carried a bundle of sacred stones with them, according to legend. These sacred stones are considered to be the physical remnant of the Sky Heroes immortal souls. As such, they are considered sacred objects to be preserved and protected. As they engaged in their world creating activities, the Sky Heroes often disappeared into the ground on which they camped or died, making these places important ritual sites for later generations of aborigines, according to Cowan (1992).

Such sacred places are known only to the tribal elders, those who have passed through the rites of initiation and transformation. The sacred objects are stored in sacred storehouses, usually caves, openings in rocks, or hollowed out trees. Like the relics of saints, these sacred objects are an important part of sacred rites and pilgrimages.

The sacred carved and painted stones are in the aboriginal spiritual centers because it is believed they were made by "divine hand" (p.108) and are filled with spiritual power. They can only be handled by elders of that spiritual clan, and they are never revealed to women or non-initiates. It is as if these sacred objects represent a direct spiritual link with the Dreaming and the spirit of the Sky Heroes (Cowan, 1992).

The aborigine is more intimately identified with his Dreaming ancestor than with his biological parents; his conception is believed to be the product of the wishes of these ancestral beings, the Sky Heroes, to bring man into a more complete spiritual wholeness.

The life-long and life-giving relationship predisposes the man to accept his unique identity here on earth. When a man finds he shares spiritual identity with another, these men become brothers, as when Chris says to David, "…because of your dream and my dream too, I brought you here" (sacred aborigine site).

When Chris and Charlie ask David to tell them about his ancestors, Chris speaks of something he calls, the *Law*. The Law refers to pre-literate aboriginal tradition that relies on intellectual and imaginative contact with their sacred constructs. Regarding this, Bill Neidjie, an aborigine (Cowan, 1992, p. 97) says, "No matter we die but that Law (tradition)…you got to keep it. You can't break Law. Law must stay."

Part of aboriginal tradition involves the myth of the Lightening Brothers, which is carried on through story and song. During their mythic battle rain comes in the form of the "rainbow serpent" (rainbow) while frogs travel with the rain. The early part of the film is filled with imagery characteristic of this traditional myth. This imagery highlights the start of David Burton's transformation, a kind of prologue to the rites of initiation in his own individuating journey.

November, the month in which the film begins, is in the middle of their season (October-December) which comes in hot and dry, then changes to rain and flooding. Aborigine tradition views this as a good time. It marks the start of David's Dream Journey.

The Dream Journey has two levels. One level is the outward Dream Journey, which follows a seasonal movement. It is more of a social activity in which all family/clan members are encouraged to participate. The other level is a more personal activity, a journey embarked on alone so that the individual might experience a clearer understanding of his spiritual nature.

The Individuation of David Burton

In a way, films can be similar to working with dreams. If different people are looking at the same film, they may see different things at different times. Art films, like dreams, involve archetypal or universal themes. Universal themes never wear out; the longer we sit with them, the deeper and more broadly we can delve into them.

As I was looking at *The Last Wave*, the theme that most impressed me and what I chose to study is David's attempt at individuation. I chose this primary theme because his individuating process, a universal one, would be an interesting way to explore the theme of opposites inherent in the individuating process, a theme which apparently intrigued both Carl Jung and Peter Weir.

Behind the opening credits of the film, an aborigine is painting on the roof of a cave, which opens like a large mouth. A black hand, protruding from a Western coat sleeve, completes a curious design, three concentric circles with four dots in the center, a central motif occurring throughout the film. This scene visually sets the stage for the theme of opposites, in which the mysterious influence of unconscious material on the Self unfolds.

Underlying Themes

One way to view David's process of individuating is through the framework of four underlying themes:

(1) the conscious versus the unconscious; (2) missing personal parents; (3) division of self-image into opposites; and (4) rites of passage and rebirth of the underdeveloped side of his psyche. Visually present in the opening scene is an overt theme of opposites revealed as black versus white (black hand in Western coat sleeve); primitive versus civilized (cave painting by aboriginal man in Western garment); and spiritual versus material (spiritual painting by man in Western garment). These underlying themes of opposites are symbolized in the film characters by Chris (tribal aborigine) versus David (Western lawyer).

Conscious and Unconscious

The theme of the conscious versus the unconscious permeates the film. David is introduced to us in the film as a successful Western lawyer, very much in his conscious ego in his roles as father, husband, and lawyer. The surfacing of unconscious material is first evident in the dream sequence in which David sees the shadow of a primitive man outside his window in the rain. He sees the figure but says to his wife, "It's just a dream."

"It is a vital necessity for the unconscious to be joined to the conscious. Nothing endangers this connection more in a man than a successful life; it makes him forget his dependence on the unconscious" (Jung, 1967, p. 298).

In the next scene, David confides to his stepfather, "I haven't been sleeping well." His stepfather asks, "Problems at the office?" David replies, "I've been having bad dreams." His stepfather recalls aloud, "You used to have those terrible dreams when you were a little boy – nightmares. You use to worry your poor mother and I sick."

In the following scene, David's stepfather continues, "I remember one night not long after I married your mother. You came to me and told me you were afraid of going to sleep at night because, you explained, as a very serious little boy, when you go to sleep people come and steal your body."

Both men laugh uneasily, and David questions, "Did I say what kind of people?" His stepfather responds that taxi drivers on night shift took him on a long ride to another world and returned him the next morning. Jung says, "Apparently it is the hostile demon who robs him of energy, but the actual fact is it is his own unconscious (1967, p. 299).

Approximately ten scenes later, David sees a vision outside the window in the rain. The figure, an aboriginal man, appears inside the house holding out a small stone with a design on it, similar to the one in the opening scene of the film. A few scenes later, David is meeting with the aboriginal defendants and, with shocked realization, he discovers that Chris, one of the defendants, is the man from his dream vision.

That evening David returns home and tells his wife about the incident and that he has invited Chris to supper. When his wife asks him if he'd told Chris about seeing him in the dream, he replies, "He just nodded as though it was quite an ordinary thing to say." Chris arrives for supper, unexpectedly bringing with him, Charlie, another aboriginal man.

During the evening, David asks Chris directly, "Are you and Charlie tribal people?" Chris responds, "No tribal people in the city." He then asks David to show them a family album. David points to a photo and says, "This is my stepfather. He's a minister. And my mother – she died when I was still a little boy. Both my parents are dead."

As David proceeds to show him a picture of his mother's grandfather, Charlie points to a carving over the doorway in which the grandfather is standing, and Chris asks, "Where is your clan territory? Noting that David seems puzzled, Chris continues, "From sunrise to sunset?"

David responds, "From sunrise, from South America. I was born there. Why is he so interested in mother's grandfather?" "He's interested in you," says Chris, "We are nothing but the Law learned from our forefathers."

Chris asks David to describe the stone he saw in his dream; then David asks, "What are dreams?" Chris tells him, "Dreams like seeing, hearing, talking, the way of knowing things. Like if my family's in trouble, from dreaming they send me messages. Dream is a shadow of something real."

Jung says, a person's real individuality is always present and makes itself felt indirectly if not directly (p. 138). Through understanding of the personal unconscious, the conscious mind becomes "suffused with collective material which brings with it the elements of individuality" (Jung, 195, pp. 138-139). Throughout David's individuating journey his conscious mind becomes "suffused with collective material" from the unconscious.

Personal Parents

Personal parents are missing in David's life. Both parents are dead. We do not learn anything more about his father. His mother remarried and died while he was still a child. As a child he experienced dream premonitions of his mother's death. We learn that he does not remember or has repressed the memory of those dreams.

At the start of the film we see David, whose superior function is thinking, with an underdeveloped feeling function. He appears to be able to access his function of sensation (concern with observable facts) better than his function of intuition. The underdevelopment of his inferior functions may have been exacerbated by the loss of his mother following his dream premonitions.

Jung says, "No man can change himself into anything from sheer reason; he can only change from what he potentially is (Jung, 1967, p. 236). Repression of those dreams connected with the death of his mother may have prevented him from mourning her loss, particularly following the early loss of his father. Developmentally, early loss of his primary attachment figures may have made it more difficult for the Self to develop as a totality of the psyche.

To help make his way in the world, David was left with his stepfather, a minister (Western spiritual leader), who, when David says he is in trouble, responds, "Do try to get it into perspective. You lost the case, but you haven't lost the world."

Agitated, David retorts, "Haven't I? I've lost the world I thought I had – the world where what you just said meant anything. Why didn't you tell me there were mysteries? You stood in that church and explained them away."

Having "lost" the world he knew, his thinking becomes transformed. At this point his superior function begins to take second place to the totality of his life. It is during that conversation that his stepfather tells him, "When your mother died, for a whole month before – you dreamt it. And what you dreamt…happened."

Divided Self-Image

When the film opens, David Burton reveals his persona, the "mask that feigns individuality…a compromise between individual and society as to what a man should appear to be" (Jung, 1959, p.136). His persona is of the rational, successful lawyer and family man.

Early in the film, we become aware of the "seeds of individual development in the guise of collective fantasies" (p. 139), the dream visions that come up from David's unconscious. The aim of individuation is "no less than to divest the self of the false wrappings of the persona on the one hand, and the suggestive power of primordial images on the other" (Jung, 1959, p. 144).

As David's dreams become more prominent and distressing to him, he is assigned a legal aid case for aborigines accused of murdering another aborigine called Billy. After meeting with several of the defendants for the first time, he says to Annie, his wife, "They're keeping something from me. One of them says he knew Billy only slightly. Another says they're old friends."

Annie responds, "Perhaps they're tribal aborigines." To which, David rationally says, "Don says there aren't any tribal people in the city." "Maybe he's wrong," replies Annie. Annie represents the part of David's Self that has been split off. He hears her expression of feelings and intuition, and they guide him further inward toward his whole Self.

Jung states that the regressive content conceals itself in many symbols, some masculine and some feminine. "...differences of sex are at bottom secondary and not nearly so important psychologically as would appear at first sight. The essence and motive force consist in an unconscious transformation of energy"(Jung, 1967, p. 429).

That night directly after his conversation with Annie, he experiences his first dream vision about the aborigines. The following day, puzzled by the growing strength of his feelings, he proceeds to question the bartender who was on duty the night the murder took place and reads about tribal killings as well.

As David becomes more and more obsessed with the case and with mysteries that are entering into his consciousness, Annie says to him, "I don't know you anymore." Gradually, he begins to trust his intuition and feelings more and more, following up on his intuition with as much factual information as he can about the aborigines, the crime, and tribal law. We begin to observe the emerging power of his intuitive function as a kind of spiritual principle in his journey.

Rites of Passage and Rebirth

The film's opening scene, with the aboriginal man

in a Western garment painting his dream journey on the roof of a cave, signals the start of David's journey of individuation. In outward form, David is the hero defending the downtrodden aborigines in the murder trial. The spiritual illumination involving the emergence of unconscious opposites is closely linked to this outward journey.

Jung describes the hero as "the protagonist of God's transformation in man" (1967, p. 392). Seven men join together on this hero's outward journey, six aboriginal men, the five defendants, and Charlie, the tribal spiritual leader. David embarks as the seventh member of the "clan."

Jung says, "In the language of initiation, 'seven' stands for the highest stage of illumination…" (1974, p. 137). In principle, this would mean that the process of integrating the personal unconscious was ending and the collective or societal unconscious would be opening up.

From the opening scene of the film, the camera cuts to a parched scene. Suddenly, without warning, rain, then wind and hail, burst from a cloudless sky, fertilizing the earth and signaling David's spiritual rebirth to come. The pouring of water continues into David's suburban home that evening from a mysteriously overflowing bathtub and the continuing storm outside. David's response to these events involving water, wind, and a shadow figure outside his window is a pensive one.

David's two daughters, Sophie and Grace, are portrayed as two little free spirits dancing, often playing in costumes as if spontaneously trying on many roles, with free access to all parts of themselves. Their playfulness is in direct contrast to David's persona. His dilemma is increasingly about the failure of his rational side to find satisfying answers to the mysterious natural events.

Following the scene in which Annie is playing with Sophie and Grace while David and his stepfather are uneasily discussing David's childhood dreams, thunder clouds appear. Rain pours down as the precipitating events resulting in the court case are revealed. First we observe Billy, an unsuccessful aboriginal initiate, running away after stealing sacred stones from the tribal sites beneath the city. Another man appears, saying, "You stole our things. You die."

The scene that follows is the fight among the aborigines outside a bar. Billy tries to run away. He stops and stares at an aborigine in a car, who is chanting softly while pointing an aboriginal death bone at him. Later at the morgue, the medical examiner is talking about the cause of death and saying, with a puzzled expression, "Heart stopped beating...not enough water to drown him."

David's invitation to the outward trials and tests of the initiate begins with a phone call while David is playing tennis. David says to the caller, "How are you going to ruin my Sunday?" The caller asks

David to take on the legal defense of the aborigines accused of Billy's murder, despite the fact that he is not a criminal defense attorney.

The evening after David's first meeting with the aboriginal defendants, more signs of regenerative transformation occur in the form of torrential winds, rain, and frogs. These signs precede the dream vision of Chris holding out the sacred stone stolen by Billy. Later, black rain falls on David's windshield as David approaches Charlie's home.

Inside, the heart of the individuating journey becomes evident when Charlie asks in a chant-like manner, "Who are you? Who are you? Who are you? Who are you? Who are you?" "Are you Mulkrul" (race of ancestral spirits from the rising sun)? "Yes," responds David. As David comes out of the hypnotized state, Charlie says, threateningly, "Don't speak in the court."

More heavy rains follow the meeting with Charlie. Driving home, David even sees water flowing from his car radio. At home, he tells Annie that she should leave the city along with the children. When Annie questions him about what is going on, David replies, "I don't know yet, but I'm frightened Annie."

His wife and children's flight from the city signals the start of David's solitary journey to integrate the totality of his Self. The literal and symbolic trial takes place in which David risks Charlie's wrath by trying to get Chris to reveal the tribal connection to Billy's death. Faith in a higher spiritual power appears to have been stirred up in David, giving him the strength to risk Charlie's wrath and the antipathy of his colleagues with his defense strategy.

After the court trial is over, David is frightened and alienated from the rational, material world he has known. Additionally, he says to his stepfather, "I've been taken with some sort of elements, and I don't know what to do. We've lost our dreams. And they come back, and we don't know what they mean."

The rites of passage continue as Chris suddenly appears at his door with the sacred stone. He takes David down underneath the city, through the sewers, to the sacred tribal site. In a symbolic way as well, David goes down underneath the city to touch his lost spiritual life.

Before leaving David in the sacred cave, Chris gives him the sacred stone and tells him, "Down there past the snake, you will find what you're looking for." The snake symbolizes the core of the transformational act (Jung, 1967). David examines the cave wall paintings which, with the spiritual, intuitive side of himself that he now accepts, he interprets as foretelling the end or death of one time cycle and the rebirth of another.

In the cave he sees the spirit mask of the Mulkrul, a mirror image of his own face and experiences the threatening presence of Charlie in ceremonial paint. David becomes frightened and grief-stricken when he discovers the entrance is locked, and he can't return the same way. Symbolically, he cannot return to his persona.

Painfully, David struggles to find another way back to the world. He emerges from the subterranean regions, psychic as well as physical, through a huge tunnel, a symbolic birth canal, out into the light – reborn. He walks out on the sand towards the ocean, washes his face in the water and looks up at a giant wave as the film ends. David Burton's ascent into the light signifies, as Jung (1967, p.359) suggests "a renewal of the light and hence a rebirth of consciousness from darkness."

Summary

Fictional characters, carefully conceived and well developed, can clarify theoretical principles, enhancing the study of human psychology. David Burton serves as an example of an individual in mid-life, who redeems himself from his persona (rational mind cut off from his intuitive function) through the healing power of the archetypal images from the collective or societal unconscious. The ending "signifies the conjunction of conscious and unconscious, the transcendent function characteristic of the individuation process" (Jung, 1967, p. 433).

References

Cowan, James. (1992). <u>Mysteries of the dreaming: the spiritual life of the Australian aborigines</u>. Dorset, England: Prism Press.

Jung, C.G. (1973). <u>Answer to Job</u> (R.F.C. Hull, Transl.). Princeton, NJ: Princeton U. Press.

Jung, C.G. (1974). <u>Dreams</u>. (R.F.C. Hull, Transl.). Princeton, NJ: Princeton U. Press.

Jung, C.G. (1967). <u>Symbols of transformation</u> (R.F.C. Hull, Transl.). Princeton, NJ: Princeton U. Press.

Jung, C.G. (1959). <u>The basic writings of C.G. Jung</u> (Violet De Laszlo, Ed.). New York: The Modern Library.

Kass, Judith. (1979). Peter Weir. <u>Movietone News, 62-63</u>, 2-8.

Weir, Peter. (1977/1991). <u>The last wave</u>. Santa Monica: Rhino Home Video.

Part III: *The Breakfast Club*
Director: John Hughes

Stereotypes and Group Behavior

"You see us as you want to see us –in the simplest terms, in the most convenient definitions, as a *Brain* an *athlete,* a *basketcase,* a *princess,* and a *criminal.* Correct? That's the way we saw each other at seven o'clock this morning." This is how the *Brain* introduces their group's narrative in the film, *The Breakfast Club* written by John Hughes.

This discussion examines the role of "leaders" in the development and cohesion of a group of five teenagers, with seemingly nothing in common except for their stereotypical views of each other, who are faced with spending a Saturday together in detention. To begin this psychological exploration, I first address the role of stereotypes as conceptualized in social psychological research, as a base from which to consider the members of the Breakfast Club. From this foundation, I will discuss how social psychology conceptualizes group development in *The Breakfast Club* by applying a modified version of Ariadne Beck's theoretical model to the group's narrative in the film.

The Brain's introduction acknowledges, at the start of their story that the teacher, as well as each group member, has categorized the teenagers as stereotypes. Implicit in his statement is his own categorization of authority figures, initially represented by the teacher on detention duty, as adults who do not see teenagers as individuals, but instead as interchangeable with other teenage stereotypes. Social psychology provides some explanation as to how stereotypes such as these develop and serve a function.

Stereotypes are shared beliefs about persons, usually personality traits but often also behaviors of a group of people (Lyens, Yzerbyt, & Schadron, 1994). Before social psychologists used this term, the word, stereotype was actually coined in 1798 and referred to a plate cast from a mold of a typed document's surface. Psychiatrists used a similar word, *stereotypy* or *stereotypie* to describe the frequent, almost mechanical repetition of the same gesture, posture, or speech common to certain disorders.

Ethnologists and clinical psychologists may still use the term, stereotypy, to refer to routine, repetitious, rigid behaviors, while in social psychology the concept, stereotype, corresponds to stereotyped attitudes, the issue the Brain refers to when he introduces the film's narrative. Walter Lippmann (1922), an American editorialist and political thinker, introduced the concept of stereotype to the social sciences. For Lippmann, stereotypes were *pictures in our heads*; according to him, people do not respond directly to objective reality but to a representation, which they have created in their minds. For Lippmann, stereotypes also contain affective ingredients, later emphasized by psychoanalysts and supporters of social identity theory (Leyens, Yzerbyt, & Schadon, 1994).

Allport (1954) identified stereotyping as a special instance of categorization, which accentuates similarities and differences, a cognitive function that simplifies knowledge and beliefs about specific social groups. Stereotyping also serves to protect and maintain values related to distinctions between social groups (Tajfel, 1982). Stereotypes, then, involve generalizations about the typical characteristics of members of various social groups, i.e., teenagers, brains, athletes, princesses, basketcases, criminals, and authority figures.

Like other cognitive constructs, stereotypes exert strong effects on the ways we process social information. For example, information relating to a specific stereotype is processed more quickly than information unrelated to it (Dovidio, Evans, & Tyler, 1986). Similarly, stereotypes lead people to usually pay more attention to information that is consistent with the stereotypes. Research confirms this accentuation, with the result that within-group differences are minimized while between-group differences are exaggerated.

Tajfel states that at least three social functions can be distinguished relative to stereotypes. One social function he identifies is *justification* of actions planned or committed against outgroups. A second is perception of *social causality*, particularly as it relates to large-scale distressing events (e.g., unemployment, inflation, and disease), the complexity of which needs to be reduced to simpler proportions. We have observed in the 20th century, extreme and at times even horrifying examples of linking stereotypes with causality, particularly with Jews during the holocaust and with the more recent causal linking of AIDS with homosexuality. Finally, the third function Tajfel identifies is the *positive differentiation* of a social group from relevant outgroups.

The teenagers' stereotypical views of each other and of authority figures does serve the function of identity with a peer subgroup, which differentiates them with a positive value from other teenage subgroups. Initially, we observe the members of the Breakfast Club acting in the stereotypical role of each person's social identity. *Social identity* is defined as the part of an individual's self-concept that comes from the knowledge that s/he belongs to a social group with positive value and emotional significance.

Even when there is no explicit conflict or competition between groups, there is a tendency toward in-group-favoring behavior, resulting from the need to preserve or achieve this positive group distinction, which in turn, enhances a positive social identity for group members. We see this playing out in everyday occurrences in team competitions. Social identity serves a particularly positive role during adolescence as a kind of safety net in teen movement toward normal developmental separation and individuation.

As well as highlighting the importance of social identity in the film, stereotypes also serve the function of *justifying* why one cannot associate or even speak to someone from an outgroup. This is demonstrated in the film, after the group has developed some cohesiveness, when the Brain asks the other group members, "What's going to happen on Monday when we're all together again?" With the exception of the Brain and the Basketcase, the others admit that their closeness will end.

Although social identity with their respective peer subgroups remained during the film despite the developing cohesion, social psychological studies by Cummins and Lockwood (1978) point to the importance of such natural situations, in which "criss-cross" individuating effects may occur. Evidence from anthropological field studies have shown that "crossing" the membership of groups, so that some individuals find themselves belonging to one group on the basis of one set of criteria and to a competitive or hostile group according to other criteria can potentially decrease negative effects of stereotyping (LeVine & Campbell, 1972). For example, the "criss-cross" effect of the teen subgroups in the film may possibly diminish the negative effect of stereotyping in the future without diminishing their own social identities.

Development of Group Cohesion

In social life in general, as within almost any group like the Breakfast Club, some individuals are more influential at times than others and may exert a powerful influence on the group. As a precursor to applying a specific framework for studying the developing cohesion of the Breakfast Club, I am going to discuss how social psychology conceptualizes leadership. For social psychologists, leadership is the process through which a member of a group influences other group members toward group goals.

Kirkpatrick and Locke (1991) have suggested that certain characteristics or traits contribute to a leader's success. From their research, they propose eight important characteristics: drive, honesty, motivation, self-confidence, cognitive ability, expertise, and flexibility. Drive is described as the desire for achievement, observed in the Athlete and the Brain. Honesty develops at different individual levels throughout the film as trust and cohesiveness develop in the group. Ironically, the Criminal is one of the leaders in openness when he "tells it like it is" as he roleplays his father and himself in contrast to his roleplay of Brian and his father.

Motivation, the desire to influence others, appears early in the film through the characters of the Athlete, the Criminal, and the Brain. Self-confidence in one's own abilities is seen in individualistic ways in all of the characters. The

Criminal is adept at "shaking up the system." The Athlete is confident in his physical prowess. The Princess is confident in putting on makeup and being popular. The Brain is confident in his academic skill, and the Basketcase seems confident in her creative ability, as she adeptly produces a sketch.

According to researchers Zaccaro, Foti, and Kenny (1991), flexibility, the ability to match one's style and behavior to the needs of followers and the demands of the situation, may be a particularly important trait for leadership effectiveness. We see flexibility operating in the ongoing development of the Breakfast Club. The film brings to life different types of leaders and the various roles they take on at vital phases of the Breakfast Club's developmental story.

Fiedler's contingency theory (Fiedler & Garcia, 1987) predicts that task-oriented leaders will be more effective than relations-oriented leaders under conditions of either low or high situational control. In contrast, relations-oriented leaders will have an edge under conditions in which situational control is moderate. If this theory holds true for the Breakfast Club, we might expect task-oriented members (likely to be male, based on Eagly and Johnson's (1990) research) to be more effective since in one sense, there is high control in that they are all confined and have to complete the essay task while at the same time, there is low situational control because in actuality, the group is left to develop its own leaders from within.

Research has revealed mixed findings regarding leadership style and approach. It appears that most people prefer a participative style, even where theory might recommend an autocratic approach, such as is attempted by the teacher on detention duty. The Breakfast Club, itself, develops in a participative style.

Since Beck's theory has been integrated with the social relations model as a tool for group psychotherapy research, Beck's model appears to have the potential for bridging the gap between group leadership in social psychology and in psychotherapy. With that in mind, I have chosen to discuss group leadership as part of the development of cohesion in the film applying Beck's model.

Beck has proposed a model for the evolution of group structure that proceeds in a systematic manner characterized by developmental phases (Beck, et. al., 1983). Each phase presents a different set of group-level issues and individual-level issues and is characterized by the emergence of leaders essential to the group's continuing development. Emerging leadership roles include task leader, emotional leader, scapegoat leader, defiant leader, along with a non-leader role (Dugo and Beck, 1984).

Although Beck has identified nine phases of group development, Dugo and Beck (1984) state that four phases (I, II, IV, & V) are relevant in issues of intimacy and hostility. These issues are particularly important in the development of the Breakfast Club, since it is composed of individuals, each of whom represents a different stereotype. Beck's phases are viewed as contexts in which the individual member has opportunities for bonding with others and differentiating self from others, while emerging leadership roles propel the group forward in its cohesion. Two main vantage points are presented in each phase: (1) the group as a whole and the fluidity of leadership roles in its development; and (2) individual level issues.

As in Chomsky's transformational grammar, we observe at the outset of the film's narrative, that the group has both a "surface" structure and a "deep" structure. On the surface, we have a group gathered together by the teacher as task leader, who directs the teenagers to write an essay describing in "no less than 1000 words, who you think you are." Looking at the group's deep structure, we initially see a leaderless group, with the teacher and the custodian wandering in and out during the course of its development.

However, for the purposes of this study, I am going to limit my focus to the deep structure, i.e., the development of cohesion of the leaderless group of five teenagers. The goal of the group in Phase I is to agree to work on becoming a group (Dugo & Beck, 1984). With development of the group as the task, we see the Criminal challenge the appointed task leader, the teacher, which simultaneously is a challenge to the group's status quo. Although the Criminal is defiant and hostile, he serves to shake up the surface system by rebellion and creating the potential for future restructuring and bonding.

Through the Criminal's "attacks," the group level issues surface, i.e., the initial identification of each of the members and their limits and expectations. Some individual issues surface in this first phase, such as "Can I accept or tolerate this group?" The Princess articulates this concern clearly when she raises her hand and says to the teacher, "I don't think I belong here." For the Brain, the issue of "Can I survive or live in this group?" is observed as the Brain stops taking off his jacket when the Criminal nonverbally "threatens" by "staring him down."

For the Basketcase and the Criminal, the issue is "Can this group accept me?" The Basketcase engages in ostentatious behaviors, such as flinging the sandwich meat up to the ceiling, and the Criminal defies the social establishment (represented by the Princess and the Athlete) to accept him when he engages in his most repulsive behavior. As the Criminal raises the challenge to the surface task leader, the Brain says, "Ah, excuse me fellas, I think we should just write our paper." When the Criminal defiantly opens the door to the room, the Brain responds in another attempt to lead the group in the surface task, "The door is supposed to stay open." The Athlete also reacts with, "That's school property; you should really fix it" when the Criminal removes a screw from the door.

Toward the end of Phase I, we observe what Dugo and Beck (1984) characterize as a strong impulse to establish a bond in terms of their common experience. We first observe this when the teacher storms in saying, "Who closed the door?" The Athlete, now leading in the task of becoming a functional group, asserts, "It just closed sir." The Princess follows his lead a bit later with, "Excuse me Sir, why would anyone want to steal a screw?"

During this first phase we observe some early signs of emotional leadership in the Athlete when he seems to experience the pain of other group members; we observe him defending the Princess from the Criminal's harassment of her, and when he says to the Criminal, "He (Brian) has a name." The Athlete begins to become an overseer of the bonding process by giving expression to the members' concerns.

As Phase I gradually blends into Phase II, the group's deep structure goal is the establishment of a group identity and direction; one of the important group level issues is around the stereotypical relating (Dug & Beck, 1984). We observe this dynamic when the Criminal harasses the Princess by asking about membership in school clubs, and the Brain interjects with the clubs he's in. The Criminal then says,

"What are you babbling about?" He responds, "What I said was I'm in the math club, the Latin club, and the physics club." When the Princess says disdainfully, "Those are academic (not social) clubs, while the Criminal comments, "But to dorks like him, they are."

During Phase II, we see the Brain emerging as the scapegoat leader, as he models and mirrors the conflict in relationship building between self-assertion and conformity. On the one hand, he conforms and tries to be a peacemaker with the Athlete and the Criminal; on the other hand, he asserts what he believes to be the task, and at another point in the film, he questions why they are following the Criminal down the hall. During all this, the group is exerting negative pressure on the Brain's differences. In keeping with Beck's model, the Athlete, as emerging emotional leader, never leads the attack on the Brain when he is emerging as scapegoat leader.

Phase III is a continuation of Phase II in that the members further explore who they are and who each of the others are; at the group level, it is a further exploration of group identity and the direction in which the group will move. The Athlete asks the Princess about a social event, which leads the Princess to reveal feelings about her parents, saying, "They're both screwed; I don't think either one of them gives a shit about me." With this, the Princess becomes a task leader when she initiates honest communication about parental conflicts, an issue important to all members. The Athlete experiences the start of significant change when he realizes that the Criminal is being abused at home and senses that the Criminal, too, is experiencing pain. Beck considers this part of the emotional leader function during this phase.

The goal of Phase IV is the establishment of intimacy, including group level issues such as coping with sexuality (observed with the Criminal's inappropriate early advances toward the Princess), expression of tenderness and coping in the group (reactions of members to the emotional stories of the Brain and the Athlete), and space for play and fantasy in the group (during and after the pot smoking). Individual level issues involve variations of the group level issue and the issue of "Can I trust?" and "Will I be trusted?" They look through each other's photos in the process of breaking down the stereotyped roles and later share their deep feelings about the events and issues that brought them to this group.

The Criminal (John), the Princess (Claire), and the Brain (Brian) smoke a joint and get high together. The Basketcase (Alyson) joins the Athlete (Andrew) and Brian, after the camera has captured Alyson following Andrew with her eyes in prior scenes. Apparently angry, Alyson leaves them. Andrew follows her saying, "Hey, you want to talk? So what's wrong, what is it? Is it bad? Real bad?

Parents?" She responds, "Yeah." He asks, "What did they do to you?" Almost at the level of a whisper, she admits, "They ignore me." In this scene we see evidence of tenderness being expressed as well as early ways of dealing with attraction.

Later in this phase, honesty around sexuality and sexual issues begins to emerge after the bravado and defensiveness. In Phase V, intimacy is deepened through the emotional sharing of the events that brought them to this group. An emotional high point is reached when Andrew admits, sorrowfully, "I tortured this poor kid 'cause I wanted him ('my old man') to think I was cool." This emotional leadership helps members to discover that they can work together more safely in the group, allowing the ones who are most fearful of closeness to consider participating more freely

The closeness and open expression of liking in Phases IV and V imply a mutual commitment. Mutuality is explored as Brian says, "I consider you my friends. I'm not wrong, am I?" With this he addresses the group issue of whether their new found closeness will continue after today.

Beck, et. al. (1983) hypothesize that after the sixth phase of group development, the roles "seem to dissolve" and the members share the various leadership roles in "more fluid ways" (p. 144). The fluidity of leadership functions and development of a "more even playing field" in the group is made apparent with the shift to first names, which continues throughout the remainder of the film, more clearly elevating each member from a negative stereotype to the status of a real human being, deserving equal respect despite their differences. Later in the film, Claire takes on the task leader function when she says, "Brian, are you gonna write your paper? And well it's kind of a waste for all of us to write the paper, don't you think?"

Brian accepts the task of writing the essay for the group as a whole. Alyson leaves with Andrew's school letter after they kiss goodbye, and Claire gives John one of her diamond earrings after they kiss goodbye. During this time, Brian is writing the group's essay. Brian's words point, not only to the dissolution of the negative contents of their stereotypes but also, indirectly, to the fluidity of leadership functions that has allowed them to develop cohesiveness as a group.

Dear Mr. Bernard:

We think you're crazy asking us to write an essay telling you who we think we are…

But what we found out is that each one of us is a Brain, and an Athlete, and a Basketcase, a Princess, and a Criminal…

Sincerely Yours,
The Breakfast Club   (Hughes, 1985/1990,
                                   final narrative scene)

References

Allport, G.W. (1954). <u>The nature of prejudice</u>. Cambridge, MA: Addison-Wesley.

Beck, A.P., Dugo, J.M., Eng, A.M., Lewis, C.M., & Peters, L. (1983). The participation of leaders in the structural development of therapy groups. In R.R. Dies & MacKenzie (Eds.), <u>Advances in group psychotherapy: Integrating research and practice</u> (pp. 137-158). New York: International Universities Press.

Commins, B., & Lockwood, J.C. (1978). The effects on intergroup relations of mixing Roman Catholics and Protestants: An experimental investigation. <u>European Journal of Social Psychology</u>. <u>8</u>, 383-386.

Dovidio, J.F., Evans, N., & Tyler, R.B. (1986). Racial stereotypes: The contents of their cognitive representation. <u>Journal of Experimental Social Psychology</u>, <u>22</u>, 22-37.

Dugo, James M., & Beck, Ariadne P. (1984). A therapist's guide to issues of hostility viewed as a group-level phenomena. <u>International Journal of Group Psychotherapy</u>, <u>34</u> (1), January, 25-45.

Eagley, A.H. & Johnson, B.T. (1990). Gender and leadership style: A meta-analysis. <u>Psychological Bulletin</u>, <u>108</u>, 233-256.

Fiedler, F.E. & Garcia, J.E. (1987). <u>Leadership:</u> <u>Cognitive resources and and performance</u>. New York: Wiley.

Hughes, John. (1985/1990). <u>The breakfast club</u>. Universal City, CA: Universal City Studios/MCA Home Video, Inc.

Kirkpatrick, S.A,. & Locke, E.D. (1991). Leadership: Do traits matter? <u>Academy of Management Executives,</u> <u>5</u> (2), 48-60.

LeVine, R.A., & Campbell, D.T. (1972). <u>Ethnocentrism: Theories of conflict, ethic attitudes, and group behavior</u>. New York: Wiley.

Leyens, J., Yzerby, V., & Schradon, G. (1994). <u>Stereotypes and social cognition</u>. Thousand Oaks, CA: Sage.

Lippmann, W. (1922). <u>Public opinion</u>. New York: Harcourt & Brace.

Tajfel, H. (1982). Social psychology of intergroup relations. <u>Annual Review of</u> Psychology, <u>33</u>, 1-39.

Zaccarro, S.J., Foti, R.J., & Kenny, D.A. (1991). Self-monitoring and trait-based variance in leadership: An investigation of leader flexibility across multiple group situations. <u>Journal of Applied Psychology,</u> <u>18</u>, 837-851.

About the Author

The author is a former University Professor with a Ph.D. in Clinical Psychology as well as a Ph.D. in Speech and Higher and Adult Education. She has taught at S.U.N.Y. Albany, The College of Saint Rose, University of Northern Iowa, University of Louisiana, California State University, San Francisco State University, The Professional School of Psychology, and the City College of San Francisco. While teaching, she maintained a private practice in clinical psychology in San Francisco. Dr. Wells is the author of professional books, professional journal articles, and published poetry. Originally from Haverhill, Massachusetts, Dr. Wells grew up in New York and currently resides in San Francisco. To learn more about her next book, contact the author at drbevwells.com or check her author page on Amazon.com.